the lavender haze

june bates
SAPPHIC POETRY

Trigger Warning
Brief mentions of homophobia and sexism.

Other Books By June Bates
she is the poem: sapphic poetry

ISBN: 9798358792579

For the girls
who fall in love
quickly & often.

the
lavender
haze

the lavender haze:

the high and the heights
sweetness and hunger
the blooming part
love's equivalent to spring
reaching for her hand
            in front of everyone
                        without thinking

I was drowning.
I was choking on my life.
I was under water for years before I met you.

it wasn't exactly
love at first sight
but it was something
like that.
the first time we spoke,
i felt it.
an ache.
like a little electric burn.
i felt my life change.

-*because of you.*

spent all summer in her passenger seat
with a playlist she made on repeat
dizzy from something other than the heat
i still keep dreaming of her hands on me

"I don't want to be your friend," she said.

Oh, right. of course. because why would you—

"I want to be more."

if you want to be my lover,
you must be fearless.
stand at the cliff's edge with me.
i want you to feel it.

the rush
right before you give in.

i want you, i want you, i just fucking want you

she broke into my heart
before she ever worked up the nerve
to touch my hand.

it was her laugh that really did me in.
it had me seeing stars and questioning sin.

i fall asleep
holding a pillow,
pretending
that it's you.

is it worth it
to risk the friendship?
what if it could be love?
what if it's not enough?

this is it, okay?
this is the moment.
there's no turning back.
nothing is ever
going to be the same
again.

i need you to kiss me.
i can't go another day
this hungry
or this crazy
or this preoccupied
by the simple thought
of your existence.
please.
i will beg like a dog
if you ask it.
i need you to kiss me.

every love poem
ever written
is about you.
i swear it's true.
i went back
and convinced
every poet
to change
their muse.

abandon gentleness.
touch me like you have been
waiting for it your entire life.
like we're burning stars
and our time's up tonight.

when i was sixteen,
i felt everything at once.
i was a dying sun.
i was a hurricane
out of season.
i was a wrecking ball
that nobody
knew how to love.
not even me.
there were years
i stayed alive
purely out of spite.

you were the first person
to look at the state of my life and say,
baby this is not good baby this is not okay
but you're okay you're okay you're going to be okay
come on
we can fix this

Will she still love me after this?

How many years can a girl bite her tongue? How many years can a girl only bite her own tongue? "Mom, I wanted to tell you—"

I can already see it on her face. I think she knows.

I can feel her love slipping away. I can feel the disappointment like it's choking me. She wishes she could choke me. Stop the words coming out of my mouth. But it's an avalanche now. "I'm gay."

A pause.

"No," she says.
Quick and sharp like a knife in the heart.

"Mom? I—"

"I said no."

when i was ten
my mother said
she would rather have
a dead child
than a gay one.

now she calls
to ask
why i never
visit home.

fuck those last texts you sent.
and fuck the poems i wrote. wish i was dead.

blessed to fall hard.
cursed to fuck up and fall apart.

what is
an oldest
daughter
if she is not
a mirror
or a toy
or a tool
to be used?

my father loves nothing he cannot control.
my mother was not a woman you could hold.
i don't know what that makes me,
but it's not free
or good
or healthy.

my father started calling me fat when i was a preteen. so worried no one would want to touch me. so worried i'd never find a man to want me. couldn't just let me grow up. had to show me what he thought of women when i was eleven. i started taking a lunchbox to school with no food in it. i still can't look in a mirror without wishing some part of myself away. *god, make me smaller. god, make me smaller. god, if you love me, just make me thin enough to disappear.*

society's expectations
kill women every day
in different ways.

"You're dating her
aren't you?
You want to
throw everything
away for some
girl?
You want to
ruin your entire life
for some
stupid phase?
Do you really need
attention this badly?
This is not how I
raised you.
This is not what I
wanted for you."

BUT IT'S
WHAT I WANT
FOR ME.

he was a nice boy, but

i wanted storybook love. i wanted fireworks.
i wanted the world and i wanted someone
who was willing to give it to me. i wanted the
big escape. i wanted the dream. i wanted the
grand gesture. i wanted the poetry and the
poet behind it all. i wanted daisy chains and
crossed stars. i wanted someone with a heart
that mirrored my own. i wanted what was
forbidden to me. i wanted to kiss her more
than i wanted to live.

you can't make me feel bad
for falling in love quickly anymore.
our lives could all use
a little more reckless living
in the name of love.
sure,
not everything will work out
but i trust my heart enough
to follow its lead.

show me where it hurts

and I will show you
what love can do.

morning.
you and me
in the kitchen.
with nowhere to go.
everything is light
and slow.
no longer afraid
to face the day.
there's joy
in having
room to grow.

It's October again and the leaves are coming down. It's not as cold as last year but I still call it sweater weather and so do you. We'll pretend if we have to. There's so little joy left to be sucked out of the world. We'll take it where we can get it. Coffee and cinnamon sugar cookies and new music and old flannels and inside jokes. I am trying not to watch the news. I am trying not to think of the time we have left. We should go out today. The pumpkin patch, maybe. Or the orchard. Let me pay too much for apples just to make you smile.

I stepped into the shower with her
and knew what it was to be baptized.
I have seen the light.
I have tasted angels.
Can the saints say that?
You think you've been close to God
but I've been on my knees
between her legs.

my soul
has chased yours
for ages,
through lifetimes,
through death.
i promised to always
find my way back to you.
and i haven't broken it.
and i never will.

i always feel you
here with me
despite
the miles in between.

some nights
i want to open the window
and scream,

do you still
think about me
like
i still
think about you?

i grew up with stars in my eyes and books in my hands. i spent my entire childhood making sure i was living in the real world as little as possible.

out of the closet
and through the woods,
to a magical land
where we're both understood
and the world isn't ending
and we're both in the clear
to be you and me
where we won't live in fear.

we could be heroes
but i'd rather be pirates.
sail back to my place
and pray we survive it.
let's undress your demons
and serve them all red wine.
take what you want, babe.
steal all of my time.

she is golden hour,

i am
basking in her glow.

would you love me if i were a worm?
would you love me if the earth didn't turn?
would you love me if i cut my hair?
would you love me if i moved over there?
would you love me if the lights went out?
could you love me even through my doubts?

the distance honestly sucks
and i won't try to romanticize that

but i love our phone calls
and your goodnight texts.
i love to write you little poems
in the middle of the night
so you can find them
in the morning.
i love sending you
old fashioned letters.
i love hearing about
how you live your days
so far away from me.
and of course,
i love you most of all.

rainbow emoji

every time
i see queer people in public
i want to cry.
it wasn't that long ago,
they were the only thing
keeping me alive.
i used to stare and dream
of what i'm doing now.
living out.
and living proud.

i thought i'd never
find home again
but here you are.

-chosen family.

in your presence,
i am energized not drained.
i am loved without condition.
i am seen for who I am.
and i can never thank you enough.

the lavender haze by june bates

she knows all the secrets
that i've tried to hide.
she knows everything
i didn't think i'd survive.

and she stays
anyway.

all my life
there was a loneliness,
a sadness,
an emptiness in me that could not be filled

and then i met you.

I could have had this all along.

That was the worst realization after finding you and finding myself and coming out. All those years of darkness and not understanding myself. All those long months of despair. All of my quiet suffering. I could have had sunshine instead. Lavender and milk and honey and light instead. I never knew there was another way to live until you put your lips on me.

it is not
an exaggeration
to say that
meeting you
changed
the entire course
of my life.

who would i
have been
without you?

how would i
have made it
this far?

thank you
for being
the person
you are.

My mother scoffs. "You're being ridiculous. I'm not homophobic," she says. "It just isn't the life I wanted for you. I knew it would be hard."

"Then why were you one of the people to make it the hardest?"

I've been dropping hairpins all my life
hoping a wife might follow me home,
but i wouldn't dare ask for it.
God forbid I should ask for it.
God forbid I should get what I want.

i know there's sappho on her shelf.
she always drinks her coffee iced.
she draws stars upon my wrists.
she gives astrology advice.
won't leave the house without her docs.
she has way too many books.
she always holds my hand in public.
doesn't give a fuck who looks.
she's thrown her fair share of bricks.
i think she'd beat me in a fight.
she wants to go live in the woods.
she reads her tarot cards at night.
her love is lavender and violet.
her laugh just makes me swoon.
she always cries to phoebe bridgers.
i wish i could give her the moon.

when your shiny new friends
aren't as true
as they used to be

i hope you think of me

still walking down
the golden road
of our lives

hoping to cross paths
one last time.

if I had another chance at life,
i'd do everything the same
just so I could meet you again.

-*let's not think about the end.*

sometimes this love
feels so big it could shatter the earth.
like gods must have conspired this.
like aphrodite sent us after each other.
like magic exists and it's you.
like we're soul mates in every lifetime
and everything that's ever happened
happened just so i could live
to see your face again.

no. i can't make myself
leave the house today.
i can't go to school.
i can't go to work.
i can barely raise my head up
from the bed.
some days love sits
like a stone on the chest.

12:01

it's midnight again
and you're not in my bed.
how can i sleep
with these thoughts in my head?

forevermore
until there's nothing left
until the stars have breathed their last breaths
until the universe weeps
and sweeps us all under the rug
like cosmic dust—

there will be an
us

couldn't find the perfect love poem
to show you how i felt, so
i became a poet.

the lavender haze by june bates

the sky fades from pink to purple to blue
and i think of the flag hanging up in your room
and i miss you

good love feels like sleep
at the end of a long week.
it's restorative and healing.

i am waiting for a kiss that doesn't end.

one day i swear
we'll get out
of this town
that's been
dragging us down.
we'll leave behind
the ones who can't
understand.
we'll take my car.
plane tickets.
or the bus.
but we're going
to climb out
of the boxes
they made for us
and baby
we're going
to run.

you're responsible for miracles
but you've never been an angel.

heaven couldn't choke you down
and hell couldn't contain you.

every part of me is on fire
when i catch her looking at me.

you're the kind of girl
who changes people's lives
and doesn't even realize it.
you sure changed mine.

she is the most exquisite torture.
hellfire i can put my hands on.
and i'm ready to burn.

your hand in my hand,
just for a moment,
when no one is looking.

-*the sweetest thrill.*

whatever she desires
it is my desire to give it to her

what is it called when it's more than friends but less than love? when i'd die for you but i'd also never tell you that? when i think of you before i fall asleep but i never text you to say so? what is it called when i look for you in every room but i don't walk over to you when i see you? when you kissed me twice but never really on purpose? was it crushing or just soul-crushing?

it's been a month since you moved on
but i still can't let it go.

i see your face in all my dreams
but i never let it show.

i was never lonely
when i knew you,
but i swear to fucking god
i have been lonely
every day since
you left.

are we soulmates?
or are we twin flames?
or are we just stubborn people
who couldn't get the timing right?

are we worth more than our goodbyes?

brave girls
dive headfirst
into love
because we
trust ourselves enough
to survive the fall.

i want to reach out
but i want to block you
at the same time
just so i never
have to think about
you again

i do miss you even when i say i don't.

i wish i could tell my mother everything.
i wish i didn't have to keep things from her.
i wish we could have been closer
but every day
there's more space

between

us.

we didn't end up together
but your love
still saved my life
for the longest time.

sorry to the boys i kissed
before i realized i didn't want to kiss boys.
i know i made you feel
like you could never measure up
or do things right.
i made it impossible to please me
because i didn't want you to please me.
i wanted *her*.

i know it didn't work out

but i just wanted to thank you
for being a safe place to break down.
you never made me feel like less
for feeling too much.

the first time i fell in love,
i didn't even realize i'd stepped in it.
it felt like breathing.
it came so easily.

-*childhood crushing.*

there are sharp
and broken parts of me
that i've never shown
anyone

but
i would like
to show
you.

her hand was soft and warm in mine.
i still feel it there from time to time.

the way your parents treat each other
is not what your love has to look like.

what if when we kiss, it changes everything?
let it change.

i want to be yours.
i want to belong to you.
i want your name around my neck.
i want to sleep at the foot of your bed.

my lovely girl.
her pixie face.
her body draped
in sheets of lace.

her quiet ways.
her perfect pout.
she teaches me
what life's about.

she shows me magic
every day

and never leaves me
room to doubt.

i kissed her

    and the flowers bloomed
    and the sky parted
    and life in its own way, began again.

the future we talked about
still lives in my head.
i know the color you wanted to paint
our kitchen cabinets.

in the middle of the night
all my thoughts return to you.
even when i don't want them to.

especially
when i don't want them to.

the way she looks at me across a room
makes the garden in my soul bloom.

on my darkest days,
she brought the color down.
she opened the curtains
and brought the sun around.

-she showed me the way out.

am i your sun or am i your moon?
would you give up the world for me
like i would give up the world for you?

the lavender haze by june bates

i'm not one for drama
but i'd suffer the gossip
and the news.
i'm not one for trouble

but i am one
for you.

to the girl I was:

I'm sorry
for the years you spent
in black and white.
I'm sorry for the darkness.
For the struggle.
For the ache.
For all the times
you wanted to die.
But I need you to know
that you beat it.
You slay every beast
in the tower yourself.
You survive.
You survive.

The only person you need to please in this life is yourself. The only person you need to please in this life is yourself.

"You're so dramatic. You could have had it worse, you know. We could have kicked you out. We could have cut you off. We could have—"

You vote for politicians who want me bleeding on the ground. You look past every sin in the bible except for mine. You tried to keep me in the closet. You use slurs to my face. You won't let my girlfriend in the house. You treat me like I am only human when I'm doing what you want. I will not be gaslit into being thankful you did not kill me, when you have killed me in so many little ways. I do not want the scraps of your love any longer. I can do without. You taught me that. Aren't you proud?

i wish we lived in a better time,
in a safer world,
but you're still my girl.

they say you have to hold on
to the little things,
but god

love feels so big to me.

when they cast the first stone
i'll be the brick through their window.
when they strike the first match
i'll go and strike one right back.

fuck their high horse
and their gospel, and their truth.

love is more real than god
and here's proof:

i will fight so you don't have to.

so we're at the end of everything
and the sky is falling and the thunder booms.
but i still feel safe tonight
sitting in your room.

in a world that tries
so hard to deny it,
learning queer history
is an act of rebellion.

for every book they burn,
we will write a new one.

it is brave
to live your life
out
in the open
like this,
knowing
people will
take shots
at you
every chance
they get.

i used to
hope karma
would get you
in your sleep.
now i just
prioritize
my peace.

a promise.

no tragedy for us.
no crying girls.
no funerals.
no wretched emptiness.
no sorrow.
i refuse to play my part
in shades of blue
and so do you.
we deserve better
and we demand it.
no one dies at the end.
we will have it all.
we will love like
the world is ending
and when it ends,
we will dance on the ashes
and rejoice.

let's be fools in love.
there's so little time left anyway.

in a parallel universe,
where you know
when you're going to die:

i'd wait until ten minutes before
and then i'd call you.
just to say *hello*. and *yes, it's been awhile*.

an ending
is only
an ending
if we let it be.

all the love
i put out
into the world
will come back
to me.

-*someday*.

Thank you for reading! Please review if you can spare a minute. I appreciate you so much. Thank you for taking a chance on my words. <3

Notes

titled "lavender haze" after the phrase from gay poet James Schuyler's love poem, "Sunday" (1974) which later appeared in an academic thesis at SFSU "Behind the lavender haze: a sociological study of lesbianism" by Nancy Elizabeth Cunningham (1976), and with regard to lavender being a historically queer color (see: Lavender Panthers, The Lavender Scare, Lavender Marriages, Lavender Menace, etc.)

About the Author

June Bates   is the author of bestselling poetry book, *She Is The Poem* – a collection of sapphic self-empowerment work. She's most likely to be found drinking an iced oatmilk lavender latte or cuffing her jeans or sobbing while listening to Taylor Swift. You know, the usual.

Contact her at: *junebatespoet@gmail.com*

Made in the USA
Las Vegas, NV
04 September 2024

94813951R00069